INTRODUCTION TO ELECTRICITY SUPPLY AND REGULATION IN INDIA

SIVA PRASAD BOSE

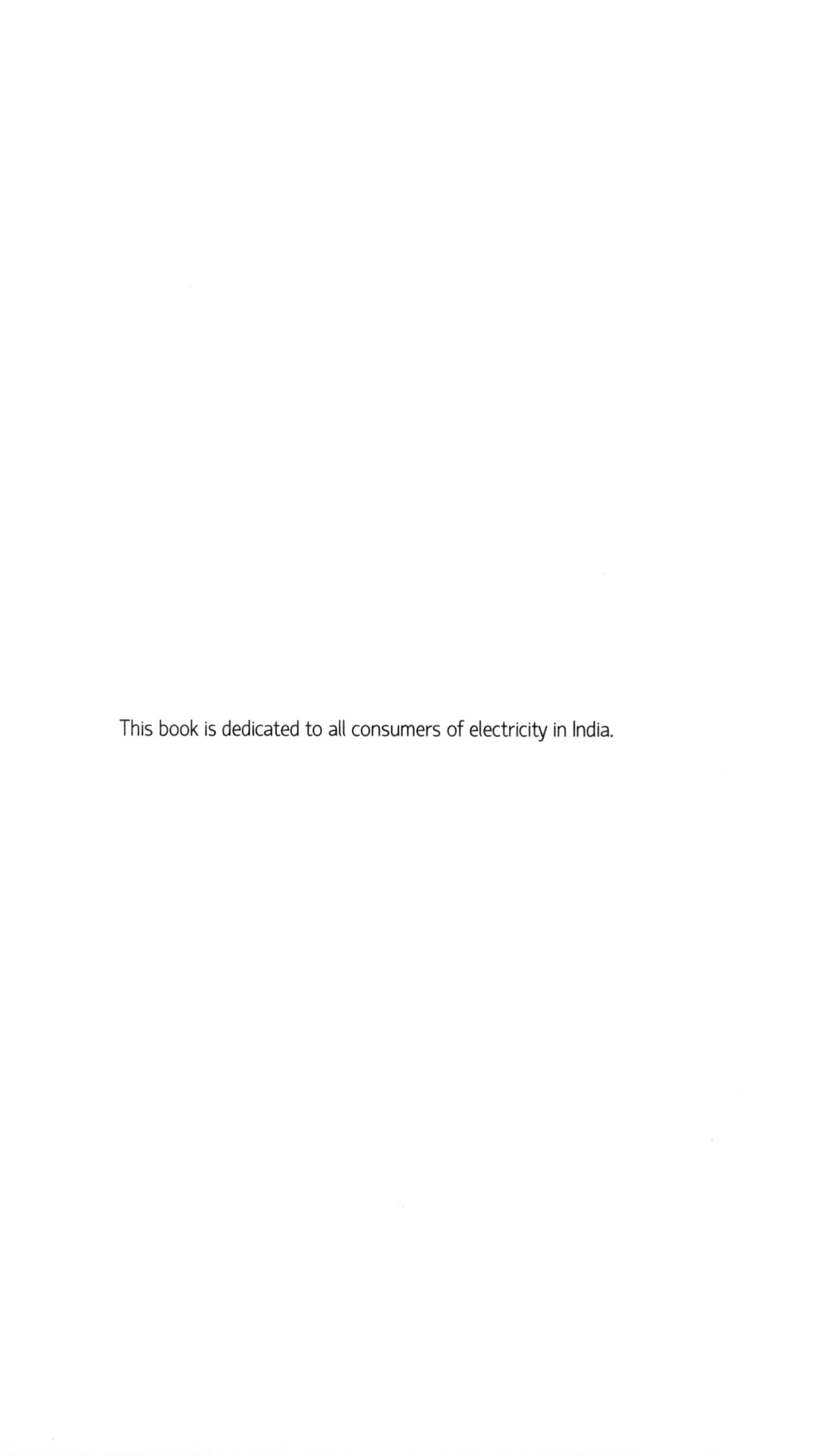

This book is dedicated to all consumers of electricity in India.

Contents

Preface

This book is an overview of electricity and power transmission aspects in India. We briefly summarise technical aspects related to the generation, transmission and distribution of electricity. We also discuss the Electricity Act 2003 in India, which is the main act regulating the electricity supply in India.

This book is divided into two parts: first is the technical part, covering technical aspects of the electricity power supply. The second is the electricity supplies laws part, dealing with the history of electricity supply, the electricity act 2003 and related matters.

It is hoped that this book shall provide some introductory guidance to those who are interested in the areas related to electricity supply and regulation in India.

Acknowledgements

The following books on energy utilization have been consulted for the preparation of the manuscript and are thankfully acknowledged:

- McGraw Hill Concise Encyclopedia of Science and Technology, Sybil P Parker, Editor in Chief
- Energy Technology: Sources of Power, Anthony E Schwaller, St. Cloud State University
- Energy, AK Bakshi, National Book Trust India
- Practical Photovoltaics by Richard J Kemp
- Newnes Electrical Pocket Book, EA Reeves
- Electrical Guide, Srikant BK Lambete, Electrical Consultant
- Thesaurus of Physics, Barnes and Noble

CHAPTER ONE

Terms and Concepts Related to Electricity Generation and Transmission

In this chapter we discuss a few basic terms and concepts related to electricity generation and transmission.

1.1 Electric Current

Electric current is the net transfer of electric charge per unit time. It is usually measured in amperes. (Mc Graw Hill Concise Encyclopaedia of Science and Technology, 5th Ed.) The passage of electric current involves a transfer of energy, since the current always heats the medium through which it passes. Most metals, electrolyte solutions and highly ionized gases are conductors.

1.2 Alternating current or AC

Alternating current or AC is the current that reverses direction periodically, usually many times per second. This is the type of current that is commonly used for public electricity supplies, due to lower losses during transmission than DC or Direct Current. Electrical energy is ordinarily generated by public or private utility organizations and provided to different types of customers as Alternating Current. One complete period, with the current flow first in one direction and then in the opposite direction, is called a cycle. The power supply in India and many other countries is at 50 cycles per second or 50 hertz, which is different from countries like USA where 60 Hz is the common frequency.

Household power supply in India is usually at 220 to 250 volts. The voltage of an alternating current can be changed by a transformer. This simple inexpensive static device permits generation of electric power at moderate voltage, efficient transmission for many miles at high voltage and distribution and consumption at a conveniently low voltage. With direct and unidirectional current (DC current) it is not possible to use a transformer to change the voltage. On a few power lines, electrical energy is transmitted at great distances as direct current, but the electrical energy is generated as alternating current, transformed to a high voltage, then rectified to a direct current and transmitted, then transformed back to alternating current by an inverter to be transformed to a lower voltage for distribution and use.

In addition to permitting efficient transmission of energy, alternating current provides advantages to the design of generators and motors and for some purposes gives better operating characteristics.

1.3 Frequency (wave motion)

Frequency, in context of wave motion is the number of times which sound pressure, electrical intensity, or other quantities specifying the wave vary from their equilibrium value through a complete cycle in that time.

The most common unit of frequency is the Hertz (Hz). 1 Hz is equal to one cycle per second. In one cycle there is a positive variation from the equilibrium, a return to equilibrium, then a negative variation, and return to equilibrium. This relationship is often described in terms of the sine wave, and the frequency referred to is that of an equivalent sine wave variation in the parameter under discussion.

1.4 Frequency measurement

Measurement of the frequency of a periodic quantity is defined as the number of times a cyclic phenomenon occurs per unit of time. The second is the commonly used unit of time. Conversely, time may be measured by observing the number of cycles occurring at constant frequency. The ordinary pendulum and household electric clocks are common examples of such time measuring devices.

The only primary frequency standards acceptable for use in the national standards laboratories for frequency reference are atomic standards of the caesium-beam type. Caesium-beam clocks have superseded other types of time measurement standards, as a consequence of the adoption of the atomic standard as the unit of time.

CHAPTER TWO

Electrical Power Generation

In this chapter, we discuss some mechanisms for the generation of electricity.

2.1 Indian power sector

India is the third highest producer of electricity in the world, having a power generation capacity of 399.467 GW as of 31 March 2022. 51.1% of the power generated comes from non-renewable fossil fuels, mainly coal, in thermal power units. However renewable energy sources such as hydroelectric power and solar power are showing an increase. India has the capacity to produce more power than it needs, although the distribution and transmission systems need to be improved.

Most of the electric power is produced in power plants, also called power stations or generating stations, that are connected to an electrical grid.

2.2 The production of bulk electrical power for industrial, residential and rural use

Although limited amounts of electricity can be generated by many means including chemical reactions (as in batteries) and engine driven generators (as in automobiles and airplanes) electric power generation generally implies large scale production of electrical power in stationary plants designed for the purpose.

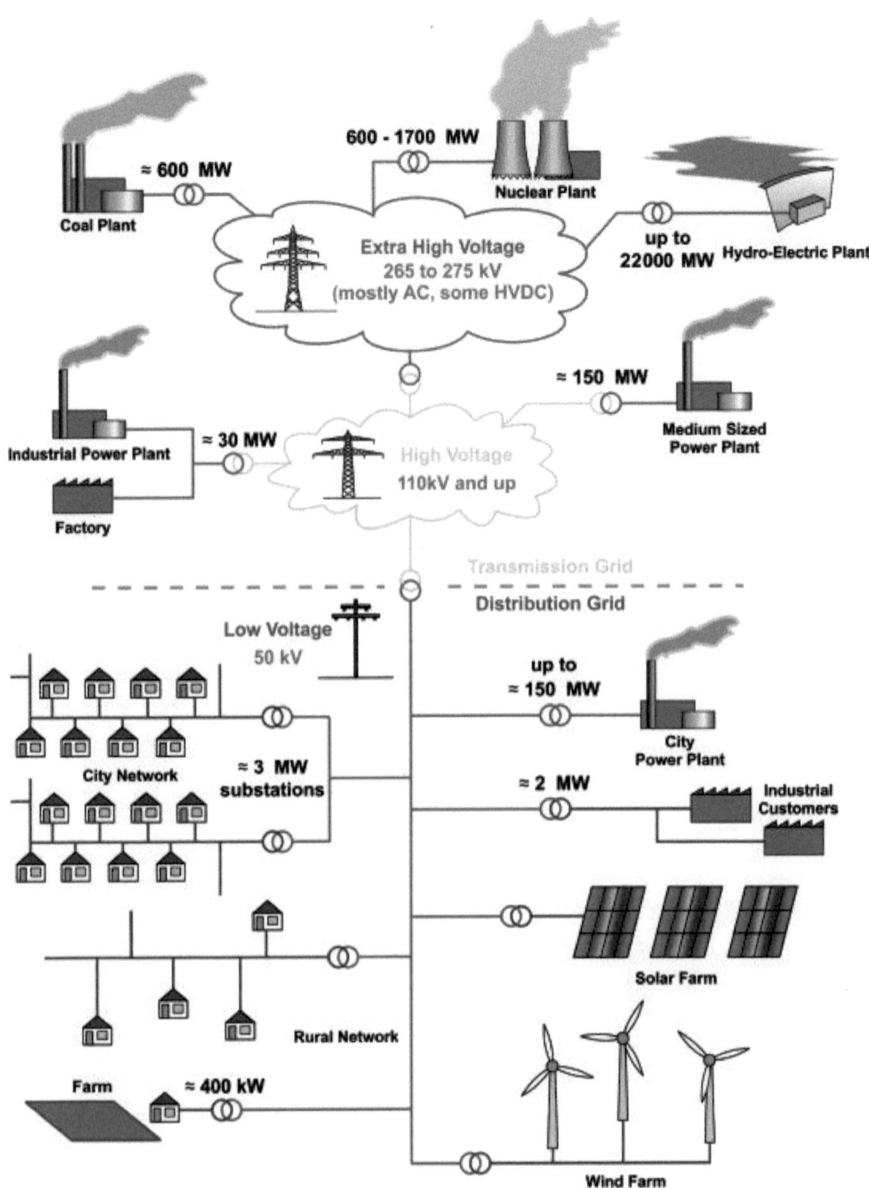

Figure: Layout of an electricity grid. MBizon, CC BY 3.0 <https://creativecommons.org/licenses/by/3.0>, via Wikimedia Commons

The generating unit in these plants converts energy from falling water, coal, natural gas, oil and nuclear fuels to electric energy. Most electric generators are driven either by hydraulic turbines, for conversion of falling water energy, or by steam or gas turbines, for conversion of fuel energy. Limited use is being made of geothermal energy, and work is progressing towards the use of solar energy in various forms. Electrical power generating plants are normally interconnected by a transmission and distribution system to serve the electrical loads in a given area or region.

An electric load is the power requirement of any device or equipment that converts electric energy into light, heat or mechanical energy or otherwise consumes electrical energy as in aluminium reduction or the power requirement of electronic or control devices. The total load on any system is seldom constant. Rather, it varies widely with hourly, weekly, monthly or annual changes in the requirement of the area served. The minimum system load for a given period is termed the base load or the unity load factor component. Maximum loads, usually resulting from temporary conditions are called peak loads. Electrical energy cannot feasibly be stored in large quantities, therefore the operation of the generating plants must be closely coordinated with fluctuations in the load.

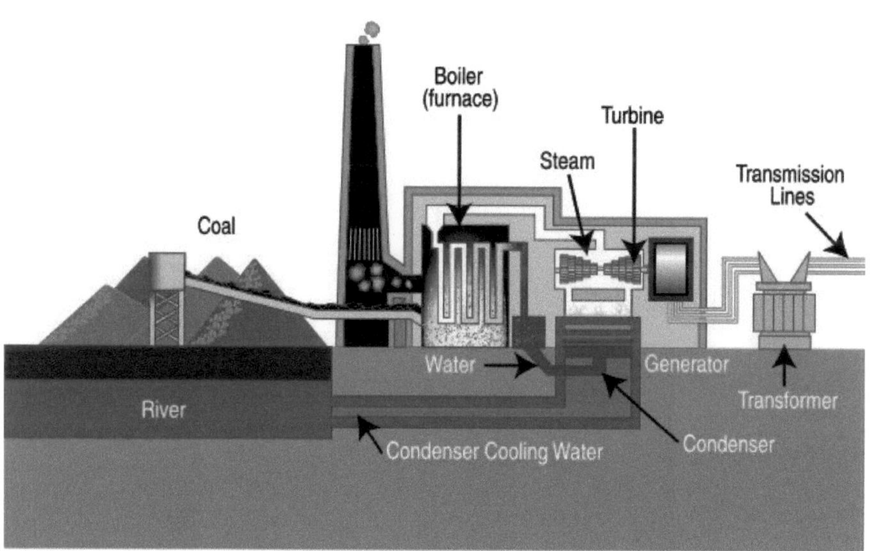

Figure: Coal-fired power station diagram. Tennessee Valley Authority, Public domain, via Wikimedia Commons

2.3 Coal power generation

In coal power plants, coal is used in a heat engine to produce thermal energy via combustion, which is then converted to mechanical energy typically through steam turbines, which is finally converted to electrical energy via generators.

In many countries the bulk of power generation is made at high efficiency coal fired steam plants, the turbo alternator sets generating power at 11 kV and with ratings around 120 mW but which can go higher till 550 mW. Pulverized coal-fired boilers are used at many generating stations, although they are being replaced with oil fired boilers since oil is comparatively cheaper.

In a coal powered generator, steam in delivered to the turbine stop valve at pressures higher than 1000 psi and 1050 degrees Fahrenheit. Even higher temperatures can be used, however these require special types of high strength steel and other engineering problems need to be addressed.

2.4 Diesel electric generation

The principle of diesel power generation is similar to coal, except that diesel is used as the fuel to run the heat engines via combustion.

Diesel electric generation has been used in some power stations but are limited to small outputs. They have the advantage of being lightweight and mobile, enabling them to be used in mobile power stations to be transported to areas where power supply has failed.

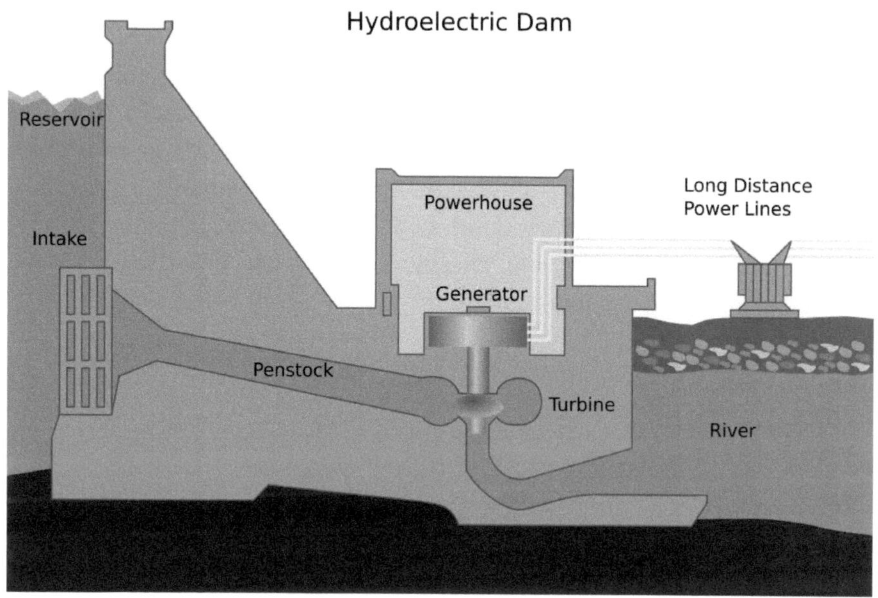

Figure: Cross-section of a hydroelectric dam. By Tennessee Valley Authority; SVG version by Tomia, CC BY-SA 3.0 <http://creativecommons.org/licenses/by-sa/3.0/>, via Wikimedia Commons

2.5 Hydroelectric power

Electricity produced from water is known as hydroelectric power.

The principal behind most conventional hydroelectric power plants is conversion of the potential energy of a dammed river into electrical energy by driving a water turbine that powers a generator.

In India, 12.3% of the total power generation or 46000 MW is produced by hydroelectricity. Major hydroelectric power plants include Koyna hydroelectric project on the Koyna river in Maharashtra, Tehri Dam in Uttarakhand, Bhakra Nangal Dam on Sutlej river in Himachal Pradesh, Srisailam on the Krishna river in Andhra Pradesh and Sardar Sarovar Dam in Gujarat.

2.6 Nuclear energy

The use of nuclear energy within our technological society is not new. The process of nuclear energy was first demonstrated by Ernst Rutherford in 1919 when he bombarded nitrogen with alpha particles to cause a nuclear reaction. Earlier, in 1808, atomic theory really developed its first foundations, when John Dalton published a book in which he discussed atoms in detail.

In 1942, Enrico Fermi along with colleagues constructed the first atomic pile which operated on a self-sustaining basis and produced a half watt of power. Soon this pile was allowed to generate 200 watts of power and thus the nuclear age had truly begun. From this point on, a great deal of nuclear energy technology developed. ideas such as atomic structure, atomic numbers, isotopes and energy were further investigated. Many scientific developments followed within a few years of Fermi's discovery.

Figure: Kudankulam Nuclear Power Plant in Tamil Nadu, India, with installed capacity of 2,000 MW. Reetesh Chaurasia, CC BY-SA 4.0 <https://creativecommons.org/licenses/by-sa/4.0>, via Wikimedia Commons

2.7 Nuclear Power

Power derived from fission or fusion nuclear reactions is known as nuclear power. More conventionally, nuclear power is interpreted as the utilization of fission reactions in a nuclear power reactor to produce steam for electrical power production, for ship propulsion or for process heat.

Fission reactions involve the breakup of the nucleus of heavyweight atoms and yield-energy release which is more than a millionfold greater than chemical reactions involving the burning of fuel. Successful control of the nuclear fission reaction provides for the utilization of this intensive source of energy, and with the availability of ample sources of uranium deposits, significantly cheaper fuel costs for electrical power generation are obtainable. Safe, clean and economic nuclear plants have been the objective o the industry's research for a while. On the other hand, critics of nuclear power demand a ban or at least a moratorium on new nuclear plants.

The inherent danger associated with nuclear power, which involves unprecedented quantities of radioactive materials, including possible wide scale use of plutonium, have been recognized. An extensive program for safety, ecological and biomedical studies, research and testing have been integrated with the advancement of the engineering of nuclear power.

2.8 Nuclear Pumped storage schemes

Pumped storage schemes are becoming more important as base load units for nuclear power stations. This means that when the demand for electricity is low, such as during the night-time, the nuclear power station generation will be used to pump water from a lower level up to a reservoir for hydroelectric power generation during the day. Such combined systems with nuclear power pumped storage schemes are used in many cities internationally.

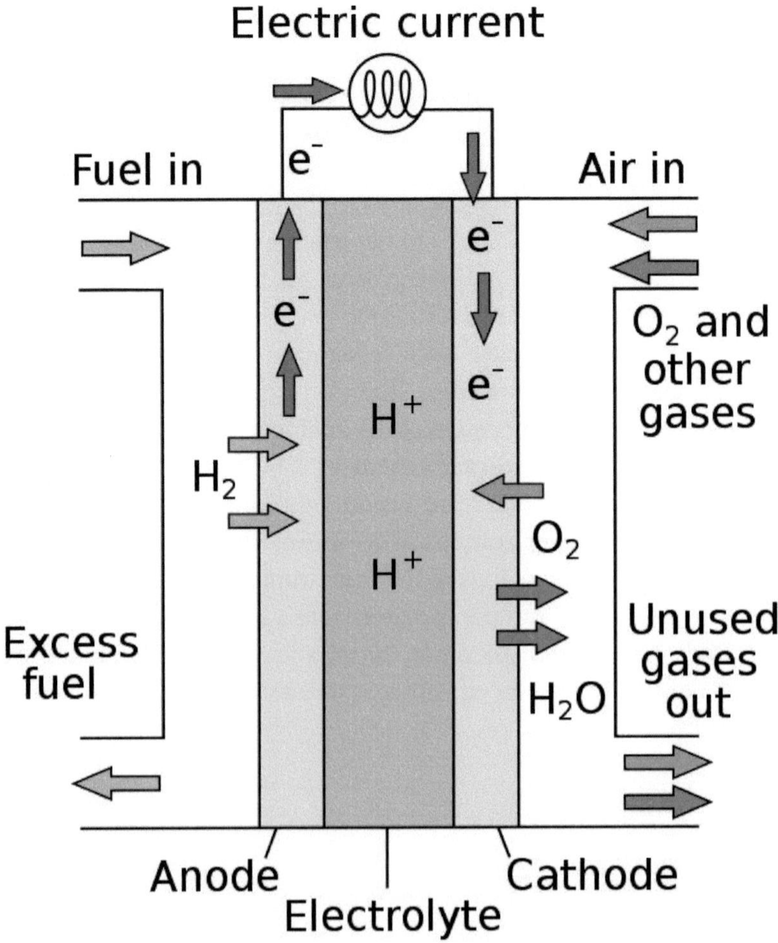

Figure: Scheme of a proton-conducting fuel cell. R.Dervisoglu, Public domain, via Wikimedia Commons

2.9 Fuel cell

A promising development in the field of power generation is the fuel cell and has been a subject of great interest. Here, electricity is generated directly from a chemical reaction. A fuel cell is an energy converter that converts chemical energy of a fuel directly into electrical energy in a continuous process. Though it was discovered over a century ago, it is the target of renewed interest because of the need to find new energy sources.

The efficiency of a fuel cell conversion of chemical energy to electrical can be much greater than that obtained by thermal power conversion, where heat is produced from the chemical reaction by combustion and then transformed partly into mechanical energy by a heat engine, which drives a generator to produce electrical energy. Further energy loss is involved if the direct current generated is converted into an alternating current or AC.

2.10 Fuel cell Reaction

Although in principle the nature of the reactants is not limited, the fuel cell reaction almost always involves a combination of hydrogen with oxygen. If the reaction is harnessed in a galvanic cell working at 100% efficiency, a cell voltage of 1.23 volts results. Fuel cells are of 200-500 Watts capacity and 50-100 mA/cm^2 current density. Larger prototypes have been produced.

In the present state of development, it is difficult to make a classification of the fuel cell types. The most successful type remains the H_2 - O_2 fuel cell of the direct or indirect type. In the direct type, hydrogen and oxygen are used as such, the fuel being produced in independent installations. The indirect type employs a hydrogen generating unit, which can be used as a raw material in a wide variety of fuel.

2.11 Chemical to electrical conversion - Fuel cell

Many exotic energy converters are being studied today, but one that is affecting a great deal of attention is the fuel cell. A fuel cell is an energy converter that changes chemical energy into electrical energy. Known for over a hundred years, the fuel cell has recently been revived due to a need to develop new energy technology. Due to the energy issue facing our society today, the fuel cell may truly be a significant part of the energy technology in the future.

Figure: Bhadla Solar Park, Rajasthan with a capacity of 2245 MW. Contains modified Copernicus Sentinel data 2020, Attribution, via Wikimedia Commons

2.12 Solar power

The principle behind solar power is the conversion of solar energy from the sun into electricity using photovoltaic cells, which are made of semiconducting materials that use the photovoltaic effect to convert light into an electric current.

Since India is a tropical country with plenty of sunlight, solar power is a fast-growing sector in India. In 2022 the solar installed capacity in India was 53.997 GW. Rooftop solar panel installations have been increasing in different states. Solar power generation facilities include the Bhadla solar park in Rajasthan, which is the world's biggest solar park in terms of generation.

References

Wikipedia. Electricity Sector in India. https://en.wikipedia.org/wiki/Electricity_sector_in_India

CHAPTER THREE

Electrical Power Transmission

In this chapter, we discuss some aspects of transmission of electricity from the power generating stations to the consumers via power transmission lines.

Figure: Electricity Power Transmission lines. Photo by Pixabay from Pexels: https://www.pexels.com/photo/cable-clouds-current-electricity-414967

3.1 Transmission lines

Transmission lines are a system of conductors, typically cables, suitable for conducting electric power of signals along large distances between two or more receivers with minimal losses and distortions.

Some examples of transmission lines are as follows:

- Commercial frequency electric power transmission lines connect electric generating plants, substations, and their loads.
- Telephone transmissions interconnect telephone subscribers and telephone exchanges.
- Radio frequency transmission lines transmit high frequency electric signals between antennas and transmitters or receivers.

Although only a short cord is needed to connect an electric lamp to a wall outlet, the cord is properly speaking a transmission line. However, in the electrical industry, the term transmission line is only used when both voltages and current at one line terminus may differ appreciably from those at other terminus.

Transmission lines are described as follows:

- **Electrically short**: if the difference between terminal conditions is attributable simply to the effects of a shunt leakage resistance and capacitance, or to both.
- **Electrically long**: when the properties of the line result from travelling wave phenomenon.

Depending on the configuration and number of conductors and the electric and magnetic fields about the conductors, transmission lines are described as open wire transmission lines, coaxial transmission lines, cables or wave guide transmission lines.

Most transmission lines are overhead or above the ground. For aesthetic reasons, some residential developments have underground distribution systems.

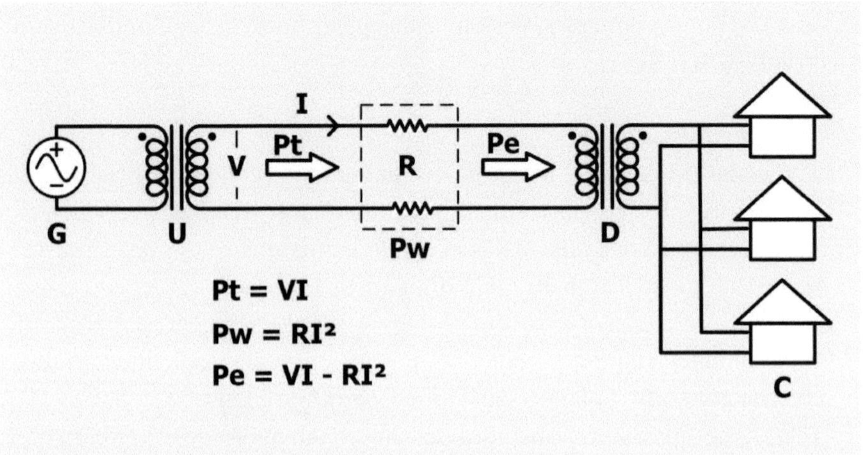

Figure: A schematic representation of long distance electric power transmission. From left to right: G=generator, U=step up transformer, V=voltage at beginning of transmission line, Pt=power entering transmission line, I=current in wires, R=total resistance in wires, Pw=power lost in transmission line, Pe=power reaching the end of the transmission line, D=step down transformer , C=consumers. Roy McCammon, CC0, via Wikimedia Commons

3.2 Theory of transmission lines

When electric power is applied at the terminus of a transmission line, electromagnetic waves are launched and guided along the line. The steady state and transient electrical properties of transmission lines result from the superposition of such waves, termed **direct waves**, and the **reflected waves** which may appear at line discontinuities or at load terminals.

In a uniform or non-tapered transmission line, the voltage or current applied at a sending terminal determines the shape of the initial voltage of current wave. In a line with negligible losses, the transmitted shape remains unchanged. When losses are present, the shape of the voltage, unless sinusoidal, is altered, because the phase velocity and alternation vary with the frequency.

3.3 Power losses

In an electric power system, the facility used to transfer large amounts of power from one location to a distant location is termed a power transmission line.

Techniques of power transmission are presented as follows:

Power transmission lines are distinguished from sub-transmission and distribution lines by their higher voltages, greater power capabilities and greater lengths.

With the exception of a few high voltage DC lines for satisfying special requirements, power transmission lines employ three phase alternating currents.

Such lines require three conductors. The standard frequency is 60 Hz/ 50 Hz. For transmitting large amounts of power over long distances, high voltages are necessary.

Standard transmission voltages are 69, 115, 138, 161, 230, 345, 500 and 765 KV. These figures refer to the nominal effective voltages between any two of the three conductors. The line conductors are usually placed overhead, supported by poles or towers, however they may form part of an underground or underwater cable.

CHAPTER FOUR

Electricity Distribution System

In this chapter, we discuss aspects of electricity distribution. After the electricity gets generated and transmitted, the last task is for it to be distributed to households and offices. This is the aspect we consider here.

The part of an electricity power system that supplies electrical energy to individual users and consumers is called the electricity distribution system.

The distribution system includes the primary circuits and the distribution substations that supply them, the distribution transformers, the secondary circuits, including the services to the consumer and the appropriate protective and control devices.

The four general classes of individual users are residential, industrial, commercial and rural.

Figure: Three-phase transformer with four wire output for 208Y/120 volt service: one wire for neutral, others for A, B and C phases. Glogger at English Wikipedia, CC BY-SA 3.0 <http://creativecommons.org/licenses/by-sa/3.0/>, via Wikimedia Commons

4.1 Three phase AC

The three-phase alternating current (AC) system is practically universal, although a few two phase and direct current (DC) systems from earlier days are still in operation. three phase transmission and sub-transmission lines require three wires termed phase conductors.

Most of the three phase distribution systems consist of three phase conductors and a common or neutral conductor, making a total of four wires. Single phase branches, consisting of two wires, supplied from three phase lines are used for single phase utilization in residences, small shops etc. Loads are connected in parallel to common supply circuits.

4.2 Distribution substation

The distribution substation is an assemblage of equipment for the purpose of switching, changing, and regulating the voltage from sub-transmission to primary distribution. More important substations are designed so that a failure of a piece of equipment in the substation or any of the sub-transmission lines to the substation will not cause an interruption of power to the load.

The primary system leaving the substation is most frequently in the 11000 to 15000 volt range A particular voltage used is 12470 volt line to line and 7200 volt line to neutral, which is conventionally written as 12470 Y/7200 volt. Some utilities use a lower voltage such as 4160 Y/2400 volts. Secondary voltages are derived from distribution transformers connected to the primary system and they usually correspond to utilization voltages.

Residential and most rural loads are supplied at 120-240 V single phase three wire systems. Commercial and small business needs are either supplied by 208Y/120 volts or 480Y/277 volts three phase four wire systems. The secondary voltage is usually used to supply multiple streetlights in addition to supplies to consumers.

4.3 Service continuity

Service continuity is the providing of uninterrupted electric power to consumers, therefore good continuity is doing this for a high percentage of the time. This is accomplished for large industrial and commercial loads by use of some form of duplicate power supply.

City commercial areas are supplied from three phase 208Y/120V grid networks. The system is arranged so that the failure of the primary feeder will not cause of loss of load on the secondary.

Commercial buildings and shopping centres are often served by spot networks. All of the transformers and protectors are at the same location.

Residential and rural loads are usually supplied by a radial system. Good continuity for them is obtained by sectionalizing the system with fuses, circuit breakers and manual switches to reduce the extent of an outage due to a failure.

CHAPTER FIVE

Electricity Supply Legislation in India and Electricity Act 2003

In this chapter, we discuss the Electricity Act 2003, which is the main law covering generation, transmission and distribution of electricity.

5.1 Introduction to the Electricity Act 2003

The Electricity Act 2003 consolidates the law related to regulate the generation, transmission and distribution of electricity in India. It also has sections related to electricity tariff and revenue policies.

It is the consolidated version of some earlier existing electricity acts in India such as the Indian Electricity Act 1910, The Electricity (Supply) Act 1948 and the Electricity Regulatory Commission Act 1998.

5.2 History of electricity supply legislation in India

The British rulers introduced electricity to India, starting from a demonstration of electric lighting in Calcutta in 1879 and a company getting the license to supply electricity in Calcutta in 1897 followed soon by Bombay. The Indian Electricity Act 1910 was one of the early laws related to the regulation of electricity supply in India. It had the provision for issuing licenses to private companies for supply to particular areas, mostly urban areas.

After India became independent, the constitution of India placed electricity supply under the concurrent list, as a responsibility shared between the central and state governments. The Electricity Supply Act 1948 was introduced. Under this act, the Central Electricity Authority or CEA at the national level and state electricity boards were set up at the state level, their job being to expand the supply of electricity to different areas within each state. These boards were all nationalized and electricity supply was a state monopoly, with licenses provided to other players by the state. Soon, the smaller towns and villages also gradually came to be electrified. However, there were problems with the electricity boards such as that of efficiency. There was extended loss of electricity supply or what was known as load shedding in many areas.

In 1991, the liberalization and reform of the the Indian economy took place. As part of this, many of the state electricity boards, many of which had inefficiencies and were in a not so good financial position, were restructured or privatized fully or partly as corporations. Private players or independent power producers were also allowed in electricity power plants such as thermal, hydro, wind and solar energy generation plants.

The Electricity Regulatory Act 1998 was set up that created he central electricity regulatory commission (CERC) and state electricity regulatory commissions (SERC) for regulating the electricity supply. These had the role of setting the electricity tariff for consumers such as households, industry and agricultural sector and also adjucating all kinds of disputes related to electricity supply. Reforms acts were brought in different states as well, such as the Delhi Electricity Reforms Act 2000 and Uttar Pradesh Electricity Reforms Act 1999.

This was followed by the Electricity Act 2003, which liberalized the electricity regime especially in the areas of electricity generation and distribution.

5.3 Background to the Electricity Act 2003

To further make the electricity supply efficient and to help with some shortcomings in earlier legislation, the Electricity Act 2003 was introduced by the government and approved in the Indian parliament. This encouraged the entry of more private players in the electricity supply and generation. The generators of electricity were free to sell the generated electricity to any customer at any location or region. This was termed as open access of the transmission and distribution of electricity.

The need for a license for most cases of generation of electricity was dispensed with. However, the distribution and transmission and trading of electricity still do need a license.

Later, the concept of customer satisfaction, consumer protection and grievance redressal in the area of electricity supply was also given prominence, and customer grievance mechanisms were instituted. DISCOMs or Electricity Distribution Companies were set up to interact with the end customers and the power generation units. State Electricity Regulatory Commissions or SERCs were also set up whose task was to prevent abuse of monopoly power by the electricity companies.

The Electricity Act, 2003

MINISTRY OF LAW AND JUSTICE
(Legislative Department)

New Delhi, the 2nd June, 2003.Jyaistha 12, 1925 (Saka)

The following Act of Parliament received the assent of the President on the 26th May, 2003, and is hereby published for general information:

THE ELECTRICITY ACT, 2003
[No.36 of 2003]

[26th May, 2003]

An Act to consolidate the laws relating to generation, transmission, distribution, trading and use of electricity and generally for taking measures conducive to development of electricity industry, promoting competition therein, protecting interest of consumers and supply of electricity to all areas, rationalization of electricity tariff, ensuring transparent policies regarding subsidies, promotion of efficient and environmentally benign policies, constitution of Central Electricity Authority, Regulatory Commissions and establishment of Appellate Tribunal and for matters connected therewith or incidental thereto.

Be it enacted by Parliament in the Fifty-fourth Year of the Republic of India as follows:-

PART I

PRELIMINARY

Section 1. (Short title, extent and commencement) --- (1) This Act may be called the Electricity Act, 2003.

(2) It extends to the whole of India except the State of Jammu and Kashmir.

(3) It shall come into force on such date as the Central Government may, by notification, appoint:

Provided that different dates may be appointed for different provisions of this Act and any reference in any such provision to the commencement of this Act shall be construed as a reference to the coming into force of that provision.

Figure: First Page of the Electricity Act 2003

5.4 Summary of the Electricity Act 2003

Some features of the Electricity Act 2003 are as follows:

- Generation of electricity is being de-licensed and captive generation freely permitted, i.e. any generating company may establish, operate and maintain a generating station without obtaining a licence under this Act with the only exception that it should comply with the technical standards relating to connectivity with the grid referred to in clause (b) of section 73. Hydro-projects, however, need concurrence from the Central Electricity Authority.
- No person shall transmit electricity or distribute electricity or undertake trading in electricity, unless he is authorised to do so by a licence issued, exceptions are informed by authorised commissions through notifications.
- Central Government may, make region-wise demarcation of the country, and, from time to time, make such modifications therein as it may consider necessary for the efficient, economical and integrated transmission and supply of electricity, and in particular to facilitate voluntary inter-connections and co-ordination of facilities for the inter-State, regional and inter-regional generation and transmission of electricity.
- Transmission utility at the central and state level to be a government company with responsibility of planned and coordinated development of transmission network.
- Open access in transmission with provision for surcharge for taking care of current level of cross-subsidy, with the surcharge being gradually phased out.
- The state governments are required to unbundle State Electricity Boards. However they may continue with them as distribution licensees and state transmission utilities.
- Setting up State Electricity Regulatory Commission (SERC) has been made mandatory.
- An appellate tribunal to hear appeals against the decision of (CERC's) and SERC's.
- Metering of electricity supplied made mandatory.

- Provisions related to thefts of electricity made more stringent.
- Trading as a distinct activity recognised with the safeguard of Regulatory commissions being authorised to fix ceiling on trading margins.
- For rural and remote areas, stand-alone system for generation and distribution is permitted.
- Thrust to complete rural electrification and provide for management of rural distribution by panchayat, cooperative societies, NGOs, franchisees etc.
- Central government to prepare National Electricity Policy and Tariff Policy.
- Central Electricity Authority (CEA) to prepare National Electricity Plan.

[भाग II—खण्ड 3(i)] भारत का राजपत्र : असाधारण 13

NOTIFICATION

New Delhi, the 31st December, 2020

G.S.R. 818(E).—In exercise of the powers conferred by sub-section (1) read with clause (z) of sub-section (2) of section 176 of the Electricity Act, 2003 (Act 36 of 2003), the Central Government hereby makes the following rules, namely:-

1. **Short title and commencement**.- (1) These rules may be called the Electricity (Rights of Consumers) Rules, 2020.

(2) They shall come into force on the date of their publication in the Official Gazette.

2. **Definitions.**- (1) In these rules, unless the context otherwise requires,-

(a) "**Act**" means the Electricity Act, 2003;

(b) "**applicant**" means an owner or occupier of any premises who files an application form with a distribution licensee for supply of electricity, increase or decrease in sanctioned load or contract demand, change in title or mutation of name, change in consumer category, disconnection or restoration of supply, or termination of agreement, shifting of connection or other services as the case may be, in accordance with the provisions of the Act, rules and regulations made thereunder;

(c) "**application**" means an application form complete in all respects in the appropriate format, as specified by the Commission, along with documents and other compliances;

(d) "**billing cycle or billing period**" means the period for which regular electricity bills as specified by the Commission, are issued for different categories of consumers by the distribution licensee;

(e) "**Commission**" means the State Electricity Regulatory Commission constituted under section 82 of the Act;

(f) "**Consumer**" means any person who is supplied with electricity for his own use by a distribution licensee or the Government or by any other person engaged in the business of supplying electricity to the public under the Electricity Act, 2003 or any other law for the time being in force and includes any person whose premises are for the time being connected for the purpose of receiving electricity with the works of a distribution licensee, the Government or such other person, as the case may be;

(g) "**days**" means clear working days;

(h) "**disconnection**" means the physical separation or remote disconnection of a consumer from the distribution system of the distribution licensee;

(i) "**fixed charges**" has the same meaning as per the provisions of the prevailing Tariff Order issued for the distribution licensee by the Commission;

(j) "**maximum demand**" means the highest load measured in average kVA or kW at the point

Figure: First page of the Electricity Consumer Rules 2020

5.5 The Electricity (Rights of Consumers) Rules 2020

The Electricity Rules 2020 were brought by the Indian government to foster better accountability to consumers of electricity in India by the distribution companies, and also include a grievance mechanism for consumer grievances. It covers areas such as connection, metering, billing and payment and the standards of performance to which the licensees (distribution companies) shall be held accountable. These rules are expected to further benefit the consumers and lead to increased accountability and transparency in electricity supply.

5.6 Conclusion

In this chapter we have gone through the history of electricity related regulation in India, and the various stages in legislation leading to the Electricity Act 2003 and the Electricity Rules 2020. We have also briefly discussed some features of the act.

CHAPTER SIX

Conclusion

In this book, we have discussed some concepts related to the generation, transmission and distribution of electricity. We have first discussed some technical concepts related to these three parts of the electricity supply.

We have also discussed briefly the history of regulation related to electricity supply in India, especially the Electricity Act 2003 and the Electricity Rules 2020, which are the main laws in India related to electricity supply regulation.

About The Author

Siva Prasad Bose is an author of various introductory guidebooks related to aspects of Indian laws. He is currently retired after many years of service in Uttar Pradesh Power Corporation Limited in Lucknow. He received his engineering degree from Jadavpur University, Kolkata and has a law degree from Meerut University, Meerut and a BSc from MMH College Ghaziabad. His interests lie in the fields of family law, civil law, law of contracts, and areas of law related to power electricity related issues.

Other Books By Siva Prasad Bose

Introduction to Wills and Probate

Senior Citizens Abuse in India

Introduction to Negotiable Instruments

Introduction to Marriage Laws in India

Neighbor Problems in India and what to do about them

Managing Court Cases with Mental Strength

Delays in Court Cases in India

Self-Publish Books and E-Books in India

Introduction to Patents and Patent Law in India

Introduction to Property Law in India

Printed by Libri Plureos GmbH in Hamburg, Germany